Usborne

Wipe-Clean

First Drawing

Use the wipe-clean pen to trace over the
dotted lines and finish the pictures. You can add
your own drawings too, if you want.

Illustrated by Stacey Lamb
Designed by Claire Ever
Words by Jessica Greenwell

Draw more bees, bugs and flowers in this garden.

Can you draw some more trees?

Draw some more boats on the water.

Trace over the dots to finish this rocket.

This planet needs some spots.

zooooom!

Finish this rocket and draw another one.

Trace over this busy digger.

Add some more
rocks and rubble.

Draw another
chugging tractor.

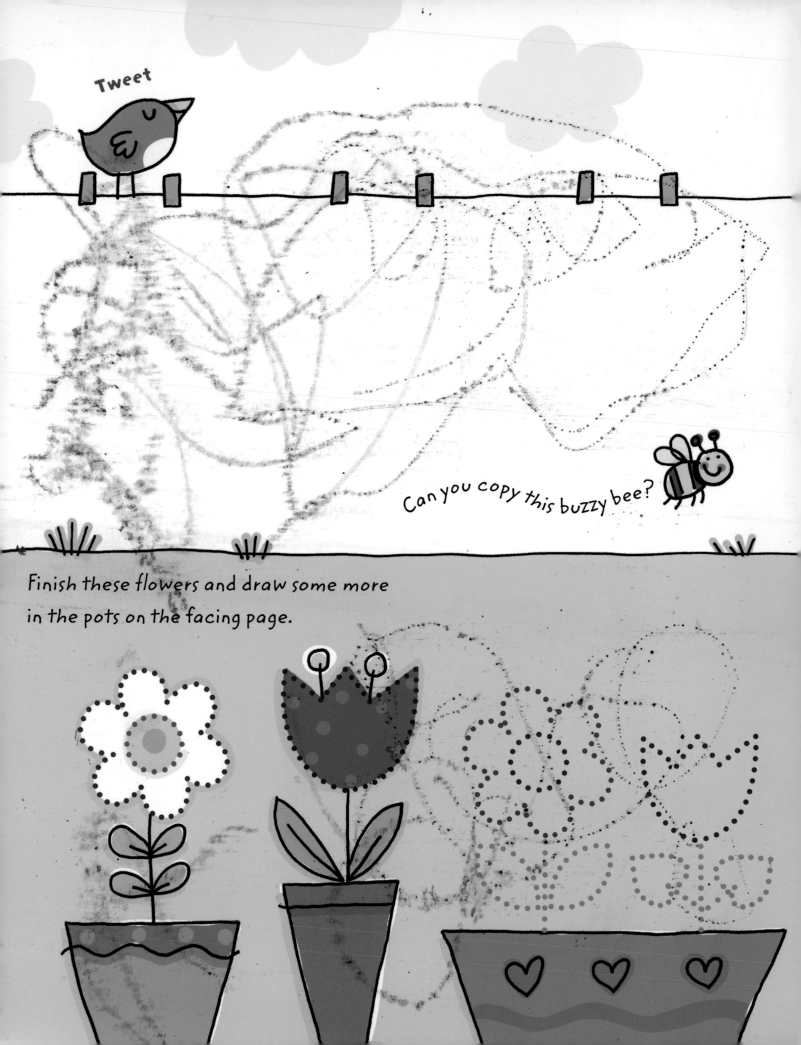

Tweet

Can you copy this buzzy bee?

Finish these flowers and draw some more
in the pots on the facing page.

Draw more of Giraffe's clothes hanging from the line.

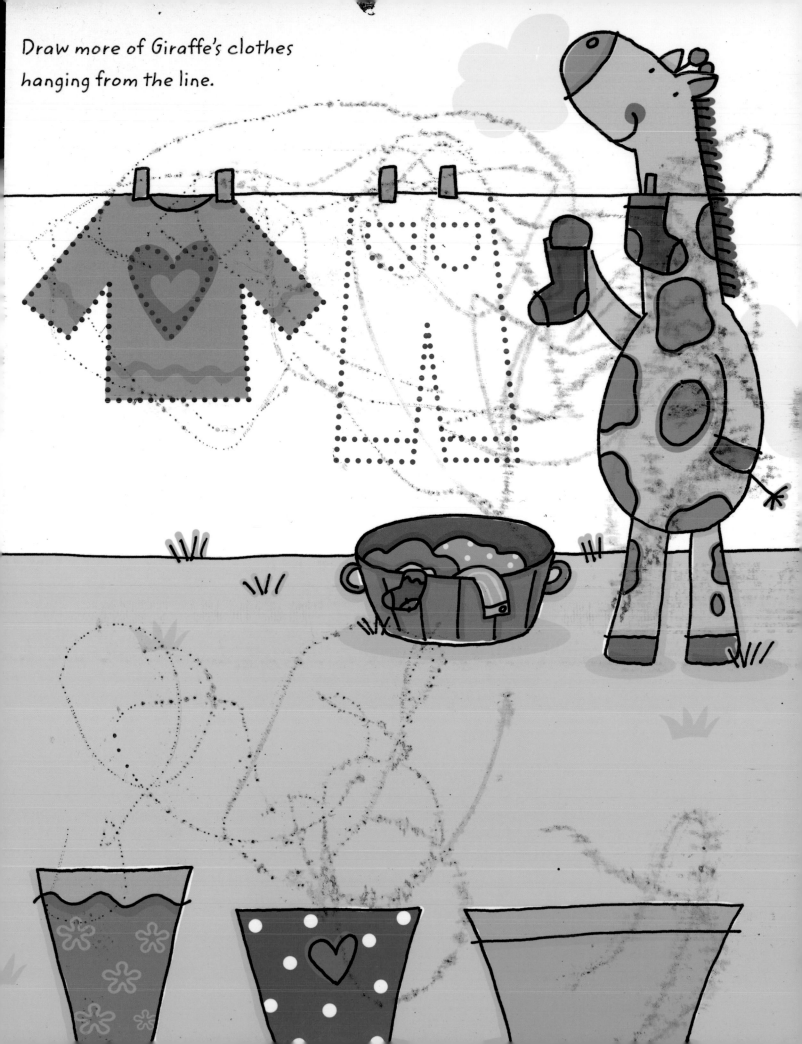

Draw some more snowflakes.

Finish this sliding penguin and draw another.

This snowman needs some snowmen friends.

This road gets very busy. Draw more cars and trucks whizzing past.

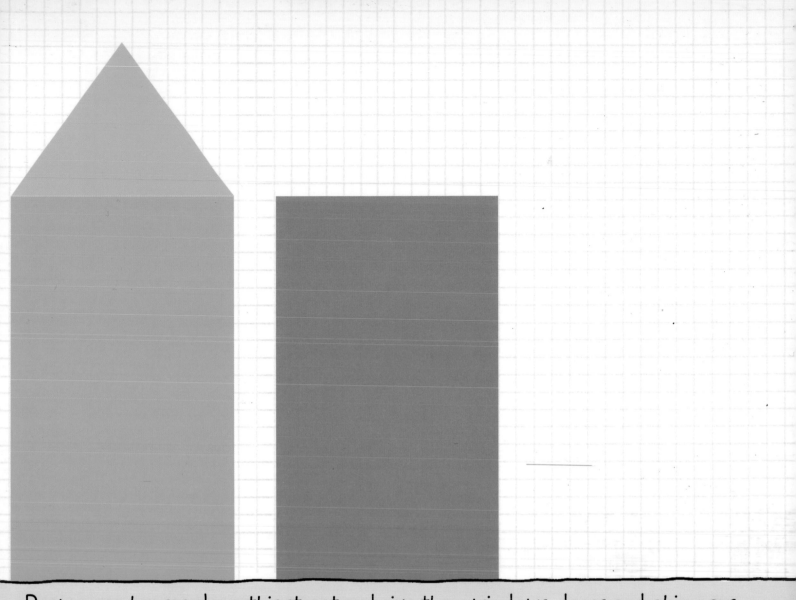

Draw more houses along this street and give them windows, doors and chimneys.

HONK!

Draw an umbrella
on the beach.